BY THE RIVER WENSUM

Also by Andrew Waterman

Living Room (Marvell Press)
From the Other Country (Carcanet Press)
Over the Wall (Carcanet Press)
Out for the Elements (Carcanet Press)
Selected Poems (Carcanet Press)
In the Planetarium (Carcanet Press)
The End of the Pier Show (Carcanet Press)
Collected Poems 1959–1999 (Carcanet Press)
The Captain's Swallow (Carcanet Press)

(Editor) *The Poetry of Chess* (Anvil Press)

BY THE RIVER WENSUM

Andrew Waterman

Shoestring Press

All rights reserved. No part of this work covered by the copyright herein may be reproduced or used in any means – graphic, electronic, or mechanical, including copying, recording, taping, or information storage and retrieval systems – without written permission of the publisher.

Printed by imprintdigital
Upton Pyne, Exeter
www.imprintdigital.net

Typeset by types of light
typesoflight@gmail.com

Published by Shoestring Press
19 Devonshire Avenue, Beeston, Nottingham, NG9 1BS
(0115) 925 1827
www.shoestringpress.co.uk

First published 2014

Copyright © 2014 Andrew Waterman

The moral right of the author has been asserted

Cover photograph by Rory Waterman

ISBN 978 1 907356 97 1

ACKNOWLEDGEMENTS

Acknowledgements are due to the following publications, where most of these poems first appeared:

Able Muse, *Acumen*, *Agenda*, *The Dark Horse*, *Envoi*, *The Frogmore Papers*, *The Interpreter's House*, *New Walk*, *PN Review*, *Stand* and *Staple*.

CONTENTS

At the Red Lion	3
Chanced Into	4
Over My Shoulder	6
Casualty, 1949	7
Those Were the Days	8
Hawthorn	11
The Philosopher and the Volcano	12
History Lesson	13
A Drop in the Ocean	14
After That Winter	16
The Asylum Seekers	18
By the River Wensum	20
In the Hereafter	22
Fairy Tales	23
The Slipper	24
A Right Royal Outing	26
Winter Postcards, Cromer	28
Catullus	30
Frankie's Acked Off	31
Day by Day	32
Still Where It Happened	36
Victim	38
Happiness	39
To Ely	41
Close-Up	43
Mioritza	46
Simferopol	50
Out of Order	51
The Examination	52
The Busteriad	54
Lost Worlds	58
The Thomas Hardy Love Poem	60
Corton	63
Quick as a Flash	64
Reading Franco Sacchetti's 'Passando con pensier per un boschetto'	66

Black and White Christmas in Verona	67
Vantage Point	71
The Letters	72
The Last Child of Empire	73
The Summer of the World Cups	76
Birthday Poem	79
This Life	81
Runner	82
Off the Brink	83
Getting There	84

AT THE RED LION

A sunlit pint in the pub garden after
another stint at the gym, for my own good
pounding a treadmill set to 'Rolling Country',
on-screen the Adirondacks coming at me,
flailed on by feel-good music; targets met.

At the old Bishops' Bridge by which they came
to the Cathedral, this is a comely building,
white-painted window-frames, Boston vine swarming
the wall. Blue sky, no leaves yet on the boughs
frittering to twigs that tap tall upstairs panes.

Suddenly three of them, ages four to seven
maybe, the girl in red, the littlest one
squealing to keep up, round and round the pub,
skipping edges, passing between me and
the board chalked *Roast Lamb, Steak and Kidney Pudding*.

A launch glides past two swans, and they've reversed,
chase anti-clockwise now, the smallest still
adrift. As children anywhere are doing,
not to hit targets, but just running. Running
for the sheer joy of it. As I once did.

CHANCED INTO

Rain on grey lake, its mountains lost to cloud,
so I turned in between two white stone pillars,
paid at the *biglietteria*. Path wound up,
the couple coming down were English, he
tapped keys to get on-screen the score
from the Oval (that was the year we won the Ashes).
They were the last of anyone I saw
or things outside the place while I was in it.

A turnstile ticked me into the tenebrous
zoological enclosure: there were five fallow deer
lifting elongated heads, the eyes
gazing back from what I had chanced into
full as the stream that pooled below us
stilling to overbrim and run-off.
Their slender legs might fire them leaps away,
but they just shifted a little, grazing.
And there were llamas, goat-kids and macaques.

Another turnstile, and above more path
under dripping greenery, suddenly opening
vistas: a glade with one great tree,
I stared into it, palm on wet rough bark,
with a thrill of recognition, here
where I had never been nor thought to come.

And higher, formal gardens,
topiary and symmetries, long flowerbanks
of azaleas, rhododendrons and red roses,
the villa with decorated balustrades.

A shut café, and the little train for children
unattended, red paint glazed by rain.
I stood by the long rectangle of pond

rich with lilies, over and over a bird
repeating its disconsolate sweet song.

Beyond all these, the finitudes
of a duke's estate surrendered now to tourists,
yet through a trick of weather lambent in them,
assuagement. Like a homecoming;
shadowing any path we take, and by
lacks gravitating to it always thwarted.

OVER MY SHOULDER

Mother, you lived so long we had time to begin.
My childhood took your love, its overcooked meals
and worries, for granted; grew to exclude you.
How can the egotism of a child know the throes of a parent?

The most naked emotion between us, fired by our shared
passion for justice, erupted in conflict.
Your politics for human improvement led you,
who'd not hurt a fly to defend the tanks crushing Prague:
They're ringed by American bases… That minefield between us.
They've housing and ballet for all. – And lock up their writers.…
Till the Soviet bubble burst, and you lived to see it,
its debris of greeds, want, bigotries, crime. And together
we grieved for ideals time slaughtered.

On these, I see other cliffs where you walked for miles,
and I twisted away, watched you dwindling over my shoulder.
Who sixty years on now break into a run as if all
withheld to the end from brief dutiful clasps could embrace you.

CASUALTY, 1949

I can't remember, maybe never knew
what I had done to make my gentle Dad
so furious: his flailing round our bedroom
lit on the battleship on the mantelpiece
I'd pasted from a silver-paper kit.
Tears burst from me as he clenched and scrunched it.

He bore no grudge, the next day in the forest,
hands in his trousers-pockets with thumbs jutting
he chipped the ball just right for me to head,
and named more trees and berries and birds singing
than I've known since, or troubled to remember.

At his tool-box he explained to me
the jittery little spirit-level bubble.
A bowl upon the kitchen dresser floated
pungent leaves, 'Your Father's medicine'.

A clearing, sunlit pond where dragonflies
glittered, a hollowed-out tree at its brink
and the cottage where the family were friends.

His suit on the straight-back chair beside his bed,
fragrant with pipe-smoke.
                            Then Mum took me elsewhere.

'Did your Dad die in the War?' I was struck speechless.

THOSE WERE THE DAYS

Mr Dupenoir is droning on about the ablative absolute,
or is it the gerund? – no matter, 'Sir sir sir!' we exclaim,
'I read in the paper a flying saucer has landed in Utah!'
Or Kansas. No matter which: Latin grammar is routed.
Another bee in his bonnet is that after the War
the British Empire and America should have gone on
to conquer the World, for as things are 'the Wussians are making
a gigantic inland sea, they plan to divert their wivers
Ob and Dnieper into it, which will destwoy ow climate.'
    Which, just now, outside the window
    pours down rain on prim South London,
    pubs and parks and privet hedges,
    chip-shops, chintz, commuter stations.

Beneath unsmiling portraits of dead Governors
and gilt-lettered honours boards, now hymns-and-Bible
routines are done with the Headmaster Mr Berthoud
('Say it,' he says, 'as in "I can't BEAR TOO much noise"')
is flogging nearly all of us, a cigarette
dangling from his lips: one stroke for every garment,
socks up to cap, through blazer, shirt, tie, scarf, that lacks
a sewn-on Cash's Name Tape. He swishes, puffs and thwacks.
    Miles beyond which, on the Downs
    Cadet manoeuvres: faces blacked
    we crawl through bracken firing blanks
    at imaginary guerrillas
    led by 'General Kash-Mai-Chek'.

Flaxen-haired Mr Fowler teaches Divinity.
When the Town Hall chimes ten we fling up our desk-lids,
pluck forth atlases and set them in the gangways,
prostrating ourselves towards West Wickham, and thus Mecca.
'Oh Mighty Allah!' 'Boys! – this paganism must cease!'
he prances around, gown flying. As when we set fire to
his waste-paper-bin and he stepped in: 'Boys! Stand back!'
    Far out in storm-thrashed Atlantic

        drifts the *Flying Enterprise*,
        only stubborn Captain Carlsen
        still on board, pig iron, coffee,
        peat moss, rags, Volkswagen cars,
        antique bassoons, and typewriters.

'Ratty' (History) has a well-stocked weapons cupboard:
chair-legs sent cartwheeling can lay a culprit out;
his bald egg-head beams as he flourishes a plank
with a nail protruding: 'Bend over!' But he'll turn it
first, and this time it's not me, sat at the back
daydreaming: Can two tigers beat an elephant?
        Other vessels gather, watchful,
        helpless as the list gets worse,
        fifty-five degrees now. Carlsen
        still won't leave his ship. In dashes
        the tug *Turmoil* and transfers
        its Mate Dancy to the wreck,
        gets a tow-line to its deck.

Scholarship-boy entrants have many things to learn.
'We don't play marbles here,' drawled a passing prefect;
and along a corridor I'm halted by the bark
of 'Rubberneck' (Doc. Taylor, Maths since Noah's Ark):
'Only erram-boys whistle,' glowering, 'am posmen.'
        All the world attends as *Turmoil*
        buffets onward through the waves,
        Falmouth, safety, are just fifty
        miles off when the tow-line breaks:
        whistles, sirens, foghorns sound
        noisily from the flotilla
        for the *Flying Enterprise*,
        honouring her going down.

Chasing sodden balls on mud, we played the game,
'Fitting you for Life!' they told us, though already
holed below the water-line the whole shebang,
flags flying and band playing, was doomed. Sank long ago.

Much more use was life itself,
happening outside the place:
biking over Shirley Hills,
friends, inventive evenings;
in time what its goings-on
totally excluded – girls,
met with in Ashburton Park,
skin between their shoulder-blades
thrilling velvet to the touch.

HAWTHORN

Again it makes me gasp, this sudden white
seethe of hawthorn in the hedgerows. More
than anything, year after year
since I was a child its apparition
declares *Live to the full, all's overbrimming.*

Again to go unused, because unshared,
without which nothing in me is completed.
I stare through frosted-glass of tears,
Ursa Major, all the constellations
wheeling fruitlessly through the firmament.

THE PHILOSOPHER AND THE VOLCANO

> *"It is indeed an Opinion strangely prevailing amongst Men, that Houses, Mountains, Rivers, and in a word all sensible Objects have an Existence Natural or Real, distinct from their being perceived by the Understanding ... For what are the forementioned Objects but the things we perceive by Sense, and is it not plainly repugnant that any one of these or any Combination of them should exist unperceived?"*
>
> Berkeley, *A Treatise Concerning the Principles of Human Knowledge* (1710)

Teetering on the crater's brink
in summer 1717
Philosophy knew what is seen
and heard (also that frightful stink),

the 'horrid gulf' emitting sound
'like thunder or cannon', 'liquid fire
consuming vines', the smoke-filled air
showering red-hot stones around

him were all in the mind, and thrilled
by his, the Immaterialist
came back for more, could not resist
such wonders: lava torrents spilled,

the Earth's gut rumbled 'like a sea
of quicksilver'... Vesuvius
shrugged, spewed out 'a sulphurous
steam' of stuff, 'surprising me'.

Leaving his notions on the shelf,
gasping for breath he made a dash
pell-mell down through rocks and ash,
so by refuting, saved himself.

HISTORY LESSON

Back in the golden age that stretched from when
squirrels could leap from the Severn to the Humber
without touching ground until saxophones and chiffon
rippling through garden parties and people saying
'Might I prevail upon you for a gasper?'

dandling brandies in glasses big as balloons
there he would be on the terrace, 'Care for a spin?'
So you tooled along in his Bentley drophead coupé
admiring the Cotswolds, and flowers arrived and one thing
led to another, you were engaged to be married.

But different things led to the skies filling
with bombs and sirens, to Nissen huts and blackout,
he went down in his Spitfire, or the *Hood*,
and centuries of ignorance went up in smoke,
and smoke curled out of death-camp chimneys.

And nothing has been learnt through the decades since
but more technology. Now we can kill the planet.
On the bit of it you still get wheeled round kids
droop jabbing text: *GR8 CU 2NITE,*
to go out clubbing, get smashed, then get laid.

A DROP IN THE OCEAN

The rubbish cart was pushed into Via Rasella
by a man disguised as a street cleaner,
and the column of German policemen came marching
through central Rome bang into the ambush.
The 16 Partisans slipped away in the crowd.

SS *Obersturmbannführer* Herbert Kappler
was quickly at the scene of the bomb, and then
in the *Generalmajor*'s office. They weighed options.
What they decided sped up the hierarchy
obtaining endorsement, the *Generaloberst* passed it
on to the *Oberbefehlshaber Süd* who passed it
to the *Oberkommando der Wehrmacht* in Berlin,
where Hitler stipulated
it be carried out within 24 hours.
A proper ratio had been calculated:
ten for each of the 28 dead Germans.

*

Some were taken from prisons, others were
previously arrested Partisan suspects,
some were picked up in Via Rasella,
in the wrong place at the wrong time.
The target, swollen by the following day,
33 policemen now having died,
was met by Kappler contributing
73 Jews he already held.

All were transported to a disused quarry
in the suburbs, the *Fosse Ardeatine*,
taken in groups of five into a cave
and shot in the back of the head.
The execution squad of officers
inexperienced in killing were provided
by Kappler with cases of cognac to calm nerves.
There'd been a small logistical blunder:

335 civilians had been brought here,
it was necessary to shoot the superfluous five
who otherwise might tell details.
Explosives buried the bodies and sealed the cave.

*

It was a murky time, a war
of liberation, and a civil war.
Straight away patriots of the Fascist kind,
and other conservatives, the bombers being
members of the Communist-dominated
Gruppo d'Azione Patriotica,
branded them unscrupulous cowards
caring nothing for Italian lives.
Why hadn't they turned themselves in?

And so through Italy's riven post-war decades.
The anti-anti-fascists shift the blame
to them, from those who perpetrated the reprisal.
Memory is a funny thing,
it goes where it is wanted, there are still
living those who see in their mind's eye
the warning posters put up by the Germans
demanding that the Partisans surrender

which never were. The Nazis' purpose, formed
in secret and carried out within a day was
terror: 'Don't touch us, or else!…'

*

All of this was only
a drop in the ocean of things we have done to each other,
but true to its element.
A deeply religious woman
who fired guns and threw bombs for the Partisans
said years later, 'Through all that time
I did not talk to Jesus.
I did not think that he would understand.'

AFTER THAT WINTER

With the equinox, a spring of sorts,
snow-melt and the river flowing fuller,
after the worst of bitter winters, when
the Spirits had neglected to protect them,
no elk herd came to spear, when the last child
died just three of them were left from thirty,
the two men gut-sick and the grieving mother.
They reasoned it out, and left their place, and headed
towards where daily the sun reached its zenith,
veering only to keep nearby to water.
On the twelfth day they chanced on an encampment,
strange tongues weighed their wary overtures
then let them stay and work. Until the cold
came back, then wanted to keep only the woman.
They left the place.
      And walked, as you could then,
so much of water being locked-up in ice
they'd never strayed enough to grasp the scale of,
across a low plain, aiming at the sun.
Weaker than sabre-tooth, they used their wits,
fashioning flints, and snares of twig and thong,
and never quite taken in by those they encountered
heard at last rumours of a fabled warm land,
its glut to hunt and pluck: 'Beyond those mountains.'
Stopping them in their tracks with mighty ice-fangs.
Against all reason. She was with child again,
they found a place. Enough to be going on with.

For twenty thousand years. Until, the miles-deep
ridged mass gargling boulders in its melt-mush
having conceded passage, over the Alps
spread villas, vineyards. Leaping where now sea was
to march straight roads right up to where they'd started.
Blank to its reason's outcomes: pushbutton slaughter,

myself here conjuring Mozart from a disc.
Cradled with *Pax Romana* and our fetid
puff of cataclysmic global warming
in a brief intermission, before Earth's next
orbital wobble brings the glaciers back.

THE ASYLUM SEEKERS

We mopped them up as they slunk from the hatch.
Grin, grin, they cooed, and were – but gesturing round
at fields, meaning the colour. They'd not say which

country they'd come from. Thousands of their kind
pay crooks to smuggle them here from all over,
fleeing rust-bucket states hoping to find

jobs and housing, health-care, life in clover.
Under our laws – I gave them chapter and verse –
you must show that, if sent back to wherever

it is, you'll get locked up, tortured, or worse,
by your regime. It seemed they'd not a notion
who ruled them, or where from. One of them burst

out spouting about heat-waves, rising ocean –
an island, it seems, less than half our size,
but all built-up, no natural vegetation

to speak of, where GM technologies
grow grapes indoors as big as tennis balls,
metre-long corn-cobs. *Sounds like paradise,*

plus night-life. None referred to death-squads, jails,
informers, stuff their sort kick up a fuss
about. Much they described was plainly false,

pure sci-fi. *I'm too busy to discuss*
this rigmarole all day, and I'm not daft,
I cut them short, *You have no claim on us.*

Their leader spoke: *You'll find your primitive craft*
are powerless to return us. And who started
climate-change, globalisation, floods? – he laughed.

The phone, our boffin: *It's got us defeated,*
that thing they came in – how it works, he said,
and what its made of. I've had it carbon-dated.

The print-out reads: two hundred years – ahead!

BY THE RIVER WENSUM

Tears smudge your syllables as on the phone
you tell me that last week your father died
during your visit home, where he'd been ill.

Tracery of winter trees
along this stretch of river-path, an angler
motionless on the bank, as ever ducks –

though which of those we threw bread to when you came
here to England still survives, I wonder,
among these rippling past today?

Flashback: I'm nine again, pressed to the pane
staring out as rain pelts garden laurels,
pierced by such greenness and a blackbird singing.

That's what goes. When any person dies
a whole world dies: first day at school, first kiss,
sunlight on the handlebars freewheeling,

certain jokes, and friendships,
that dingy street stunned into sudden beauty
by jazz flickering from a cellar grating –

the myriad disparate moments intermeshed,
configured to a singularity
no-one else can ever live in.

Here they come running now along the path,
a dozen children waving wooden swords,
'We are samurai,' they inform me.

A black dog hurtles in to bound among them,
and here is their teacher, as I suppose she is,
who tells them: 'The little dog loves you because

he knows you love dogs,' and 'Run ahead to the tower,
there you can have your ultimate battle,
but we have only five minutes.' The swords are clacking,

and some of them will never forget this moment.
This is how lives define themselves,
it is nothing to do with careers and examinations.

And I have learnt many things, yet know no more
of depths than when through streaming window-glass
I thrilled to thrumming rain.

I hope for your father that at last complete
the world he had become, which could not be
without him, brimmed into lucidity.

Turning for home as the low orange globes
of lamps come on, I stoop to look: through grass
still strewn with skeletons of autumn leaves

clusters of green blades thrust, stalks
paling to tips not swelled to buds yet, barely
divining their gold blaze as daffodils.

IN THE HEREAFTER

Forget eternity, give me just one day.
The big white house above a scoop of sea,
whin spilling gold down glen behind it.
They've all turned up… Some, fresh from a dawn swim
are mooching round the garden, its great trees,
gazebo, flowerbeds where no petal drops;
but most, back late last night from the pub
where the fiddler brought down the rafters, are inside
sipping coffees. There are no hangovers.
Dogs barking, cock-crows from a distant field,
the high whirr of a coastguard helicopter
confirm all's true, with the sun's heat
in fissured stones of this wall I lean upon.

Letting things be. So they play chess, or tennis
(swift as my thought, the courts appear),
devour the afternoon light with passionate talk.
A kindling, astonishingly become
the blaze life dreams of, nothing out of place
but, as it should be, perpetually surprising.

When evening brings all indoors, there's the party.
For you, my friends from scattered years and places,
not least those I lost track of through neglects,
sad fallings-out, or time's attrition.
Effaced among the throng, my satisfaction
is seeing how, at what for most is first meeting,
you like each other. As the moon sails out
from a hill, I slip away, to leave you talking:
books, love, jokes, blood fired, our music playing.

FAIRY TALES

The room falls silent, and the child asleep.
There's ironing to be done, a meal to cook.
Boredom bloodshot with terror (children weep)
when he reels in drunk. This is no storybook

where Cinders, Ugly Duckling, Beast, the miller's
third son, are graced by shape- or class-mutation.
On her TV, for blondes the serial-killer's
got stuck in to there's no resuscitation.

Outside, wolves gobble flesh round slum estates;
in cops' gear giants pump more volts through Jack;
Puss flees from Palace boots. Art replicates
(*Ah, mirror, mirror...*) disenchantment, lack.

On pillows, among facts bad as they seem,
If-only flames unquenched, our vital dream.

THE SLIPPER

The earliest tales had shown her the wronged child
triumphant, evil punished, sleights from hearth
to palace, wakenings. These enchantments filled

like sails of a tall ship her setting-forth.
Crossing frontiers brought more quest in view.
Such castles as still hulked across the track

proved empty ruins the rain whistled through.
Cleared of fierce beasts, the forest was pruned back.
Yet, out of reach now, the ogres crouched at screens

reprogramming the terrain: a blighted street
closed round her, where in purring limousines
wolves grew sleek devouring easy meat.

No fairy godmother: the crone who took
the cakes she offered spat at her and cursed.
Geese laid no golden eggs; no flower spoke.

What metamorphosis did occur reversed
the books': Prince Charming bearing flowers, prized her,
but, settled for, turned Beast. *You've made your bed,*

lie on it, those she counted friends advised her.
Yet still there lurked, in pages she now read
to her child, the banished vision. Till a scald

of tears woke her one night, she crept tiptoe
to the junk room: there, as the dream had told,
her long-lost slipper lay. Restored by no

royal claimant who would once have blurred its gift: *I am trust, by risking which, it glittered, only, if only for few, comes quest's reward.*

She tried it on, took first steps. It still fitted.

A RIGHT ROYAL OUTING

The Tudor gable hood and full-length dress
cluttered with geometric patterns draw
stares as she hops on, brandishing her pass.
Standing-room only? That is not her style.
The cretin slumped to his mobile with dropped jaw
and jabbing thumb rebuffs her bawled demand:
'Fuck off, grandma!' 'Off with his head!' A whirl
of stumpy sceptre topped with a squat heart
swats him sprawling down the bus's aisle.
Though this seat, ripped and stained, falls some way short
of the throne she'd lost when that appalling girl
sent her whole pack flying, and Wonderland
dissolved. Of course, when circumstances alter
one must adapt. The King, worn down by years
of coping with her, couldn't cope with that,
sat tugging his forked beard, his old wits cracked:
'But, my dear, where are our courtiers?'
She packed him off to a Home, with the Mad Hatter.
She signed on in the police force, eager
for the violence, but found she couldn't stand
the deskwork, teamed-up with sex traffickers,
became a Madam, that got more respect:
punters trembled at 'Off with their cocks!'
There'd been just one celeb-spot on the box,
in *Grumpy Old Women*, but the PC mob
squealed in outrage at her clamour for
executions. She lights a cigarette,
snuffing out sparks of protest with a glare,
alights at the stop outside the Queens Arms pub,
and stomps in yelling for a pint of lager.
It's us against the Germans in the World Cup,
when the ref disallows Frank Lampard's goal
her legs writhe furiously round the bar-stool's legs:
'Off with his head!' of course. And when they score

their fourth, her hurled glass whistles through the air
to trash the screen. There's uproar, the staff quail,
they'll not shift her at closing-time. She jogs
round the pool table smashing balls non-stop:
'It's me,' she crows, 'who makes the rules in here.'

WINTER POSTCARDS, CROMER

1

The sea-wall is dark with spray from the tidal
crash – hear the shuddering pebble-maul.
And none in any handful ever knows
what jostled us together, and will part us,
dragged aside, sunk deeper, or cast up.

2

On the clifftop the putting-green is flagless;
only a hardy few walk the boards of the pier.
Stripped of its garnish of holidaymakers
the town huddles into itself, in shops and pubs
near-empty as the great church beneath its tower
no flash or jingle of phrase, the drab coin of humour
is pisspots and parking-tickets. Don't try irony.

The heart? I think of that crab, at a touch
flinching down flush into ooze.

3

Occasionally someone, usually walking
a dog, says 'Good evening'. Is it he who,
bent raking the supermarket freezer,
twisted a creased neck griping about prices?
He has been here for ever. Behind closed doors
more happens in Norfolk than junk TV,
squabbles about doing homework: here are
murders, blackmails, arsons, incests, hauntings.
He was among those John Paston noted:

*With cuirasses, briganders, jacks, sallets,
and long trees with which they broke up gates and doors.*
Still at dusk to a passing stranger
he proffers a taciturn courtesy.

4

Now and then through the one-way system,
crazily daubed a car rips, windows
wound down, hammering bass-beat,
jumping the lights to and from somewhere
unlikely to differ. These are our settlements,
in Plonsk, Nobeoka, Oshkosh (Wisconsin),
among coral reefs or crimson parrots,
we grope for our dreams, in tide-ruck, quicksands.

5

The children will come back, their holidays tumbling
from train or car, to speckle the beach with colour,
to shrill from the boating pool where the boy who returns
again and again is given a longer go.
To squirm their toes in the tide's verge staring
at blue laced by the rasp of a zigzagging speedboat.

This, then, the Promised Land.
Never found after, nor to be doubled back to.

CATULLUS

Since that siesta when, your gut
well fed, you felt fresh hunger poke
up through your tunic and your cloak
and sought relief with a sweet slut,

or having crossed far lands to come
in mourning, tearfully you laid
the gifts brought for your brother, said
'Hail and farewell!' before his tomb,

empires and ideologies
have heaved to crest then sink like waves,
filling their myriads of graves,
and all's changed by technologies

undreamt in your ambitious Rome,
whose wreck I've strolled. And strolled also
your loved 'near-island' Sirmio
where Garda's lapping soothed you home,

though bicycles, ribbed vaults, the sonnet
were not invented when your gaze
rose to this moon, that nowadays
we've sauntered too, hit golf-balls on it.

Vivid still your Lesbia's pet
sparrow pecks her fingertips
as vows cascade from her false lips.
Your *Odi et amo* rends us yet.

FRANKIE'S ACKED OFF

      (Translated from Petrarch, *Canzoniere* CLXIV)

Nuffin stirs, sky, earf an wind keep stumm,
dawgs quits yowlin, sparrers grabs a nap,
overeads a loader stars an crap,
the sea dont give a toss; sawlright fer some,
I wikes, frets, sweats an bawls fer er oos messed
me up inside like Chinky sweet-an-sahr:
a war-zone, choked an ragin evry ahr;
an only finkin of er finds some rest.

Like from the self-sime bottle booze yer sup
at first lights up an then does in yer ead,
iss birds yer nuts on screwin screws yer up.
Strewf, aint no end in sight, I drop dahn dead
a fahsend times a die, bahnce back fer maw;
them Pearly Gates still miles off like befaw.

DAY BY DAY

(Translated from Giuseppe Ungaretti, 'Giorno per giorno')

1

'No-one, Mum, has ever suffered so...'
And the face already gone
But his still-living eyes
Turned from the pillow to the window,
And sparrows thronged the room
Around the crumbs scattered by Daddy
To distract his child...

2

Now I'll be able only in dream to kiss
The trustful hands...
And I talk, I work,
I am scarcely changed, I am frightened, I smoke...
How is it that I can bear so much night?...

3

The years will bring me
Who knows what other horrors,
But if I felt you near,
You would console me...

4

Never, you'll never know how it lights me up,
The shade that settles itself beside me, shyly,
When I no longer hope...

5

Where is it now, where is the artless voice
That running and resounding through the rooms
Raised a tired man from his worries?...
The earth has undone it, it is protected
By a past of fairytale...

6

Every other voice is an echo that fades
Now that one calls me
From the ageless summits…

7

In the sky I search for your happy face,
And may these eyes of mine see nothing else
When God wills that they also shall close…

8

And I love you, I love you, and it is an endless rending!…

9

Ferocious land, monstrous sea,
Separate me from the place of the grave
Where the tormented body
Now decomposes…
It doesn't matter… Ever more distinct
I hear the voice of that soul
Which I knew no way to protect down here…
It isolates me, always more merry and friendly
Moment by moment,
In its simple secret…

10

I have come back to the hills, to the beloved pines,
And the native accent of the wind's rhythm
That I shall not hear again with you
Breaks me at every breath…

11

The swallow passes, and with her the summer,
And I too, I tell myself, shall pass…
But of the love that rends me let not the only
Sign that remains be a brief misting-over
If from hell I am to reach some quiet…

12

Under the axe the disenchanted branch
In falling scarcely grumbles, even less
Than the leaf at the touch of a breeze...
And it was fury that brought down the tender
Form and the devoted
Compassion of a voice consumes me...

13

No longer does the summer bring me furies,
Nor spring its premonitions;
You can subside, autumn,
With your fatuous glories:
For a desire stripped bare, winter
Stretches out the kindest season!...

14

Already autumnal dryness
Has sunk into my bones,
But, prolonged by the shadows,
There supervenes an infinite
Demented splendour:
The secret torment of the engulfed
Twilight...

15

Shall I always recall without remorse
A bewitching agony of the senses?
Listen, blind one: 'A soul has departed
Still unharmed by our common punishment...'

Shall I be less cast down to hear no more
The living cries of his purity
Than to feel almost extinguished within me
The terrifying shudder of guilt?

16

In the dazzle that shrills from the windows
Shade frames a reflection in the tablecloth,
In the fleeting shimmer of a jar the swollen
Hydrangeas from the flowerbed, a drunken swift,
The skyscraper in a flush of clouds,
In the tree a little one's frolickings, come back…
Inexhaustible thunder of the waves
Imposes itself, then floods into the room
And, on the troubled steadiness of a blue
Horizon, every wall dissolves…

17

Fine weather, and perhaps you pass close by
Saying: 'May this sun and so much space
Calm you. In the pure wind you can hear
Time walking and my voice.
I have gathered little by little and closed
Within me the mute gushing of your hope.
For you I am the dawn and the intact day.'

STILL WHERE IT HAPPENED

In the Museo Archeologico Eoliano, Lipari

A heap of smooth stone balls,
size varying, excavated
from where they landed, over
two millennia
and a few steps from here.

Displayed in other cases
decorated vases
depict dance, acrobatics,
banquets, clowns and gods,
Pan finds a sleeping maenad.

Also found in tombs,
votive offerings,
is the huge collection
of Greek theatre masks,
tragedy and comedy,

characters from plays
(some lost) by Aristophanes,
Sophocles, Euripides,
mouths gaped in grief or mirth;
gold objects, lamps and jewellery;

and the terracotta
statuettes, some showing
scenes from domestic life –
a woman sews, a mother
bathes her infant child.

All coheres within
the realm of Dionysus,
god of transformations,

of wine, the theatre, and
joys in the afterlife.

Ways of being, knowing,
imperfect, sometimes cruel,
smashed by these placid stones
fired from catapults
when the Romans came.

Next door the Cathedral
rears its baroque front,
and several other churches
stand in various stages
of dilapidation

within the massive ramparts
the Spaniards built around
these heights after the Turks
sacked what had supervened
on the old acropolis,

leaving little standing
but the Norman cloister
I've strolled round, with its Doric
columns and capitals
filched from vanished temples.

I glance out of the window:
far below this cliff-top
a hydrofoil unzips
its white wake on blue sea;
now tourists gravitate here.

I turn and stare again
at this pyramid of stones,
hoarding in their slumber
dying screams and anguish,
the splintering of bones.

VICTIM

He looks again at the only surviving photo
of the mother of the prize-winning physicist
whose biography he is writing.

She is doing a handstand, blue-jeaned legs
wheeling, her face intent,
lips slightly parted issuing air.

She is very young. Was she his mother already?
The physicist does not know, at his grandparents' where
he would grow up, they never told him.

Those were troubled times, as may come again.
The village massacres, the rival armies.
Was it a bomb or a bullet? Did she have time to scream?

HAPPINESS

> For my son Rory on his wedding

Remember that day at Yarmouth?
– I watched the cone in your grip
tilting, until *splat!*
on the pavement, your world
lost… But the man in the shop
gave you another ice-cream, free.
The seaside came back.

The next year, happiness
was a tree-house, high and dry
among greenery filtering
sunlight and bird-song,
a ladder up to it and
the steel pole to slide down
to the little train that circuited
the grounds, past water.

Then came the paper boats
we folded to race on the Witham,
more fragile vessels, some
were pecked ragged by swans.

All these were a long time ago
– longer for you than for me;
that is the way time goes,
contracting as we pass it.
Teaching us loss
that knows no remedy,
settings-out that never
come round full-circle,
and how soon, as for those boats,
dissolution comes
in the shrugging welter.
And also this:
that the truest happiness

is when life finds some use for
the love we ache to give.

We cannot command it. Choosing
(as we must) may betray us.
Or, suddenly dancing
like snowflakes under a streetlamp,
it melts at the touch of earth.

Denied it, all we achieve
means only ashes,
the scald of tears.

All we can do is be ready.

TO ELY

Fields, now brown, now green,
floating past my train,
copses dense with thin
boles, neat villages.
No wilderness remains:
all's shaped to purposes.

Flower-baskets dangle
on platforms we flick by;
and regularly dissecting
the fen into rectangles
dykes are cut reflecting
blankly back grey sky –

millions of miles beyond,
creatureless and plantless,
spins Jupiter, we send
probes that beam back lightning
jagging gas-swirl. Frightening,
dwarfing us, and pointless.

Above these levels floats
Ely Cathedral, wrought
by the past's hunger for
embrace with the transcendent
rearing its lantern-tower
to the firmament.

I walk the river-path
beneath it, past trim boats,
a pub, and children throwing
bread to ducks. All knowing
what they are about,
within what stops my breath,

a cosmic fireworks show
infinitely expanding
that long before *forever*
would bore God dead although
he'd sparked it off: star-shiver,
barren, blind, unending.

Stood here at the brink
now my mind is reeling,
nothing I can think
sustains me. Water flows,
I clutch what simply shows
minute intent, this railing.

CLOSE-UP

When twilight comes it pulls the mountains near.
Keeping going, picking up after falls,
fording the rivers, had been enough to push
horizon on before me, keeping distance.
Now as a shiver passes through the grass
it closes in, looming, and no way of telling
what, if anything, might lie beyond it.

*

New-built, and fit for all its purposes:
spotless corridors ramify, lifts purr,
to where things happen, beyond the waiting areas
saccharined with wall pictures, fish in tanks.
A woman recalls sweets long gone, liquorice twist,
bull's-eyes, flying saucers, 'the Coronation
there in black-and-white on a twelve-inch screen.'
And one by one we are called, some wheelchaired on,
some helped by steadying arms.
                              'State of the art,
all our equipment here,' they tell me
as flat on my back I'm slid within
the CT scanner's glimmering tunnel, fearing
that if this thing the biopsy found inside me
has spread, this suave machine won't fail to find it.

*

'Look! – snowdrops!' cries my sister by the river
past Pull's Ferry, 'you could say
a drift of snowdrops.' Delicately surmounting
wan February grass. A year ago
Veronica rejoiced in them: 'Bucaneve!
Vedili!' – then they were adrift on snow.
Now I kneel to stare at one close-up,
the tiny flower pendant on bare stem,
supplicant, heralding spring's accession
through gold swathes of daffodils to May's

hedgerows foaming with white hawthorn blossom.
Gift annually thrilling, yet at each
recurrence piercingly unique.
That now I can't for next year take for granted.

*

As if a crash that somehow not abruptly
over carries on, no end in sight
yet caught within it visions of sweet elsewheres
clear of it. Yes, I'll come to Venice,
talk poetry drinking wine by the canals;
and to you in Taormina where
we'll linger in the public gardens among
hibiscus and bougainvillea, hearing
toc... toc... toc... from the tennis courts,
balls flying to and fro, voices calling the score.

*

As just one rotten apple in the barrel
corrupts the whole, this cancer in my... No,
that's cliché... Nor does biology know
moral categories. So let's say
a pearl, occasioned by one speck of grit,
expanding in layers round it...
      I'm away
inside my head, as head-and-shoulders clamped
to a narrow table by the Perspex mask
they beam the radiation through
my throat.
   But neither will that image do:
the pearl protects the mollusc, doesn't kill it...
Trying words for this shifts it to a plane
where I embrace it...
      'As spores inhabiting
an organism reproduce to spread...'
Hoping their rays will zap the bastard thing.

*

The view from here pulls far things close and clear:
short-trousered, Elastoplast on knees, and hair
incorrigible, a bunch forever vying
come to the stream. Rope slung over a bough,
each swings, lets go, makes it to the far side
no worse for a grazed palm or shoeful of water,
myself among them, and pushes on,
gobstoppers bulging cheeks, snapping off shoots,
whooping, reckless, vanishing
into forest… Careers, marriage, divorces,
and, these overcome, what's still to come.
Deaf to my warning cry, 'Mind how you go!'

MIORITZA

(Translation of the Romanian folk ballad)

On a green slope straight
Below heaven's gate,
Descending the trail
That drops to the vale
Come three flocks of sheep
Three shepherds keep,
One a Moldavian,
One Transylvanian,
And one Vrancean.
Now the Transylvanian
And the Vrancean,
Sharing their thought,
Conspire in a plot,
When the sun leaves the sky
The other must die,
That Moldavian,
The wealthier man,
With more sheep in his flock,
Long-horned sturdy stock,
Better-trained horses
And his dogs the fiercest.
But a ewe-lamb, small
With yellow-white wool,
While three days pass
Bleats without pause,
Won't eat any grass.
'Pied lamb with your black
Face and legs and white back,
While three days pass
You bleat without pause,
Don't you like this grass?
Are you too ill to eat,
Mioritza my sweet?'
'O dear shepherd, gather

Your sheep to the river,
Dark woods spread through
With grass for us too,
And shadow for you.
Master, master,
Call to that pasture
The bravest of all
Your dogs and most loyal,
For at sunset those two
Intend murdering you,
That Transylvanian
And the Vrancean!'
'Lamb, if by some spell
What's to be you foretell,
Should I chance on my death
On this stretch of heath,
Tell that Transylvanian
And him, the Vrancean,
They should bury me near,
In the sheepfold here,
So that I will
Be with you all still,
And hear my dogs bark
Round the fold in the dark.
Tell them what I've said,
Then place at my head
A pipe of beech,
Of love is its speech,
A pipe of bone
Caressing in tone,
A pipe of elder
Fierier and wilder!
Winds when they blow
Will sound through them so
All my sheep crowd
Round weeping aloud
With tears of blood!
But don't breathe a word
That I was murdered,

You must only say
I married today,
A king's daughter my bride,
The whole world's pride;
At my wedding tell
How a star fell;
That the sun and moon
Carried our crown;
Of the guests at our feast,
Firs and maples, our priests
Great mountains, and birds,
Thousands of birds
Our lutes and guitars,
And our torches stars!
But if you sight,
If you should meet
My old mother in her wool
Sash, from her full
Eyes the tears flowing,
Over fields going,
Asking of all,
Speaking to all,
"Who of you has known,
Who has seen my own
Proud shepherd, as slim
As if drawn through a ring,
The white of his brow
Milk-foam from the cow,
His moustache neat
As an ear of wheat,
Thick curls that grow
Like the plumes on a crow,
And his two eyes
Wild blackberries?"
Then, my little ewe,
Pity her too,
You must just say
I married today

A bride royal and great,
At heaven's gate,
But to my sweet
Mother never repeat
That a star fell
At my wedding, nor tell
Of the guests at our feast,
Firs and maples, our priests
Great mountains, and birds,
Thousands of birds
Our lutes and guitars,
And our torches stars!'

NOTE

The ballad *Mioritza* (Ewe Lamb), known by Romanians in hundreds of variants for centuries, was first written down and printed by Vasile Alecsandri in 1850. His is the standard literary form, but its creator is the Romanian people. In *Mioritza* they find a myth defining their identity and psyche. It fuses fatalism – the victim neither fights nor flees when warned of what threatens – with a transcending of evil in a manner both mystical and ethical: a majestic pantheistic affirmation coupled with, in the shepherd's instructions to his lamb, a compassionate moral vision. *Mioritza* differs from such other national epics as the *Iliad* and the *Nibelungenlied* not only in its brevity, but in its minimal narrative, dropped with its outcome undisclosed as a serene lyricism supervenes. Instead of relations between characters shaping action, here they are undeveloped beyond the jealousy of the two other shepherds; but nature, rather than mere backdrop, is an active agent. *Mioritza* has complex, mutually enriching origins; the notion of death as a wedding has been traced back to pre-Roman Dacia. Its spell is in the power and beauty of the myth, given perfect artistic shape that is no feat of individual genius, but evolved through the collective processes of oral telling. My translation aims for as close a fidelity as possible to the text and feel of Alecsandri, for which adherence to his pithy rhymed form, with its unadorned directness of diction, is essential.

SIMFEROPOL

In the gardens of Simferopol
peach-trees blossom, art and poetry
brim café talk, there is a patter
of high-heel shoes, creative keyboards, water
dropping from fountains in Simferopol.

A place, the guide-book cavils, *to pass through,*
in its Soviet-period constructivist glory.
There is one old mosque (restored). And I, who've never
been there see details zoom-lens clear:
embroidered shirts, and on a sill a bowl

of fruit, below scrubbed steps some chickens pecking.
Outside the city mountain tracks beguile
to heights that open views to the Black Sea,
as fluent and capacious as your souls.
Depths glint with the sunk freight of history.

Eyes closed, I hear four chimes: *Sim-fer-o-pol*,
as from the bell of one of its white spires.
Beneath which poems I failed years ago
complete themselves. 'Now we shall walk,' you call,
'by the river, with millions of stars up.'

OUT OF ORDER

My local pub is gradually falling into
a hole in the ground, it is subsidence in Earth's crust
which is riddled with holes like a Swiss cheese,
or bubble wrap. There was that double-decker
bus careering along along Unthank Road
that suddenly vanished, as if through a trapdoor.

The builders were to have come after Christmas
to jack the place up and pump silicon under it,
but they did not come, they are still working on costings.
It is listing more steeply, cracks zigzag down the walls.
Dave is banging on, 'It's totally out of order!'
about whatever irks him, council tax spies, speed traps,

duvet covers, 'The bureaucrats in Brussels,
"Jump!" they command, and we ask "How high?"'
Poles coming here with their work ethic, Ipswich Town
and, were he ever to glance at the sky,
you'd be adding winged Pegasus, friend of the Muses
and bearer of thunderbolts.

It won't be like the *Titanic*, orchestra playing
as we go down, and anyway we are free to come and go.
Though both the doors, one facing Tesco's, the other
towards the pet-shop now need barging open.
Stella talks of restarting Sunday lunches.
The builders talk of July perhaps, or October.

'Last orders at the bar!' There is a juddering
plunge, balls leap from the pool table
to clatter the ceiling, knocking out lights,
and flung off his stool, beer jumping out of his glass,
as he's gulped under Dave's having none of it,
he lays down the law: 'It's totally out of order!'

THE EXAMINATION

The signal came somewhere between
sensing the tricks you might work
with an opposable thumb
and mastering fire: *You can look
at the questions and begin.
Have a go at them all
within the time allowed
which depends on yourselves.* Some
hung back in caves for a while,
some showed more aptitude
than others, or had better luck:

wigwams and totem poles
didn't quite measure up
to Athens and Angkor Wat;
but problem-solving devices
from the abacus and the axe
to the zeppelin and the zip
brimmed non-stop, cannonballs
smashed castles, Foxton Locks
got boats uphill. You met
with setbacks, suffered falls,
but bounced back from each crisis.

So cities and empires spread,
with many an eye-catching wonder,
the Sphinx, the Blue Mosque, the Louvre,
Big Ben and the Hoover Dam;
you scribbled railways all over
the planet from tropics to tundra;
and your finer thoughts were distilled
by Plato, Li Po, Shakespeare, Freud,

Pascal and Omar Khayyam –
a row of tumblers to hold
the oceans of blood you've shed.

And some of the questions had been
set in invisible ink,
appearing too late, or were born
of your answers: splitting the atom
left you to juggle the Bomb.
Under your talking heads
the space that remains is shrinking,
poisonous with your greeds;
now red alert is blinking,
the virus is in the machine
and all your screens going blank.

THE BUSTERIAD

1

Enthroned in his cab atop the huge yellow Compactor
(bulldozers might be its kittens), chomping a burger,
Buster is monarch of all he surveys:
a refuse tip to horizon where Lincolnshire
flinches. He gropes rolls of gut for his mobile,
downloads *Great Beckham Freekick Goals*, then starts
the spiked wheels churning. In the rancid mulch he thwacks
are Shakespeare's *Works*, old double-beds, dead kittens.
Buster has been around a long time.

2

Buster was hiding under a bush when Falstaff
flopped feigning, and the Douglas ramped off
for other quarry. Bellies up, they squinnied
at the Prince and Hotspur exchanging dunts,
till the latter fell. 'Spare me such grinning honour,'
mused Falstaff over the corpse. 'Back of the net!'
yodelled Buster, always a patriot.

3

The first million years were the worst. Watching stalactites grow
in a cave. Buster, never in shape for the chase,
was thrashed with a mastodon bone for being useless.
Glaciers bulged and withdrew, gouging landscape,
and no-one invented shops or the caring professions.
What would he like for his birthday? He daubed it beside
their wall hunt-voodoo: a Ferrari. 'If God,'
said his mother, 'meant us to move like that
we'd be born with wheels, not legs.'

4

Pissing in the fireless grate of a drasty inn
Buster rued pilgrimage. 'Shoures soote' forsooth!
He was drenched, saddle-sore, bored numb with their tales.
The prissy Prioress, that pimply Pardoner
who'd sold him rats' bones as holy relics.
A thump sent him sprawling: 'Your turn!' boomed the Host.
'These three Irish plumbers met a Paki…' The toff
who'd talked him into the trip didn't lift his quill-pen.

5

Buster knew nothing of art, but he knew what he liked.
Not acres of dimpling boys on the Sistine ceiling.
Nor carting the Maestro's supplies up, pisspots down.
Nor their food… When he quit the Italian job
he left an eye-level graffito, *Mad Cow*,
frothed lips ballooning, *Eat Our British Burgers!*

6

Buster sat out the Armada. Shipboard stockfish
had left him no stomach for it. Not to speak of
the sight of their sails, those long-range cannon.
Kindling fireships you'd never know how the weather
might blow. He tossed his cap high on North Foreland
when it wellied the Spaniards out of the park.
Then Sir Walter sailed home with a pallid tuber:
after that it was chips with everything.

7

When Buster came round from the drubbing his mother gave him
for eating the goose that laid golden eggs, she sent him
to market. He came home with beans.
She chucked them. One sprouted right through the clouds…

You know the rest: when she kick-started him up
his weight brought it down. They were sent to the workhouse.

8

Then there was the wife. Why do women have legs?
'So they can walk from the bedroom to the kitchen,'
leered Buster. But this one, you never knew where she was.
Or who with. Bringing back watches, gowns, periwigs.
'Red-card the trull, ref!' The Beak sent her off – to Virginia.
But just as he settled, feet up and six-pack handy,
a key in the door, she reeled in ginned and bedizened,
his trouble-and-strife: Moll bloody Flanders.

9

Buster was fifteen, hardly yet quite bald,
when they sent him out to build Empire.
'Sun, sex and sherbets, son.' He had bad memories
from the Crusades: too fat to aim bows
so given a pike against mailed Saracen horsemen.
As well halt tanks. This time he was cannier,
when Zulus darkened the skyline, he shot his foot off.
Got shipped home to a desk-job in Recruitment.

10

'Blood, sweat, toil, and tears.' 'No thanks,' said Buster,
switching the wireless off. Our darkest hour?
Boom-time for the black market.
'Nylons, lady?' Clouds have silver linings.

11

Space? It takes the weight off your feet.
Buster won six golds at the Moon Olympics,
but declined orbit missions, telling his mates
in the Rat and Trumpet, 'Pints won't pour out there.'

12

Dante has Buster sunk to the ears in his element:
filth, with the gluttons in Hell's third circle.
It could be worse: the boiling-blood-bath for Violence
(too much like work), and as for those stuck as straws
within nethermost ice, you can't fault Buster on Treason.
'Did we win the World Cup this year?' The poet ignores him,
tags on behind Virgil, the voice of Reason.
'Right, but there's plenty more of me where I come from!'

LOST WORLDS

Gaslit London, horse-cabs trundling, choking through pea-souper fogs,
nose-to-ledger on a high-stool ink-stained till you pop your clogs,

or at 'Forward, Jinks!' advancing, collar chafing, to display
drapes that 'might just suit you, Madam,' priced at twice your monthly pay.

Like the sticklebacks your childhood fished from ponds in a tin cup,
circling the alien jamjar for a bit, then floating belly-up.

All very well for those off stomping tundras, deltas, sun-drenched veldts,
blazing away with guns like drainpipes, bagging moose and lion-pelts.

Beats your Sunday skulks on Penge municipal grass. What's there to lose
but what you stoop to every weekday buffing a shine on cardboard shoes?

'Yes, Professor Challenger! – deck-hand, tea-boy, take me on!'
Next thing you know your paddle's whacking water up the Amazon.

Jungle-trek to the lost plateau, get up, find Jurassic brutes.
'Sportin' risk, young fellah!' Lord John squints along his sights and shoots,

bullets bounce off, iguanodons go on chomping foliage while
Challenger scribbles zoological notes with a *Eureka!* smile.

Terrible snarls, trees snapped like matchsticks, tyrannosaurus looms,
                                                                            gives chase,
teeth like scimitars; hide in shrub, it pounds past. Challenger mops his face:

'Cranial crevice too minute for reason, we are the masters there!'
Hairy arms grab you, gibbering ape-men drag you to their skull-strewn lair.

Get away, join their smooth-skinned humanoid foes, Lord John foresees
'dooced good scrap!' Guns win, apes wiped out. Grateful cave-girl
                                                                                 on her knees,

absolute corker, flutters eyelids, love her madly for a week,
pterodactyl swoops, she's gone, legs wriggling in receding beak.

Tunnel finds escape-route down, reach coast, ship home, thank lucky stars
snug in a leather chair, smoke curling as Lord John hands round cigars.

Danger is addictive, soon you're off with Allan Quatermain,
deepest Africa discloses Twala's murderous domain:

rightful king restored, discover Solomon's Mines, the hag Gagool's
crushed by the door she slams to trap you; exit, pockets crammed with jewels.

Next there's *She*: Ayesha, beautiful merciless queen the tribe knows 'must
be obeyed' – the spell reversed, she crumbles into age-old dust.

Fugitive from 'The Country of the Blind', sometimes adventuring
heroes you guest along with perish – Dravot, 'The Man Who Would Be King'.

Meanwhile redcoats push back frontiers, capital reels the unknown in;
sundowns on far-flung verandas, ice-cubes tinkling in gin.

Round the corner, unsuspected till you're in it, Flanders mud,
technological massacre, gas shreds your lungs, you gargle blood.

'Up and at 'em!' 'King and Country!' 'Salt of the Earth!' our heroes cry.
Another shellburst, hunter Allan Quatermain is blown sky-high.

Daily deafening bombardments, from both sides the big guns fire;
in No-Man's-Land Lord John is screaming, dangling shot-through on
                                                                           barbed wire.

Haggard, Doyle, Wells, Kipling, Lost Worlds topple dead as ancient Rome.
Europe claims the title now, the Heart of Darkness has come home.

THE THOMAS HARDY LOVE POEM

I
Dear Teresa Greene,
Where are you now?
In shine, in haze? –
Or has Time's plough
Erased your blaze,
Dear Teresa Greene?

II
You, Teresa Greene,
Bent spudding docks,
Made my heart jump
To glimpse red socks
Below your rump,
Sweet Teresa Greene!

III
Sweet Teresa Greene,
Braids turnip-blonde;
Or was that Sue?
For I grew fond
Of quite a few,
My Teresa Greene!

IV
But, Teresa Greene,
You lipped the Squire,
By wealth beguiled;
Behind the byre
Were got with child,
False Teresa Greene!

V
O, Teresa Greene!
I seized your throat

To spill your blood;
Your hay-rake smote
Me flat in mud,
Spry Teresa Greene!

   VI

Shame, Teresa Greene!
Snared by gems' lure,
On dainties fed;
I sold manure
For honest bread,
Ay, Teresa Greene!

   VII

Yet, Teresa Greene,
Life's mocks prevail:
Babes choke on sweets,
Squires die of ale;
For you the streets
Gaped, Teresa Greene!

   VIII

Yea, Teresa Greene,
Still skies are blue;
My beard is grey,
I'm eighty-two
And locked away.
Woe! Teresa Greene.

   IX

Nay, Teresa Greene,
Fate may ordain
This loony-bin
Rejoin us twain –
Though long past sin,
Sere Teresa Greene!

Coda

    (Scratched through by the second
    Mrs Hardy on the poet's MS)

Now, bottoms up!
Ich toast 'ee, jades!
Zo prim in nave,
Zo lewd in glades,
Till cwold in grave.
Ar, bottoms up!

CORTON

I stare through drifts at where erosion's lopped
away the grassy tract which annually
I bounded over in the sack-race, dropped
the turf on which I triumphed in the sea.

We came here four years running in a train
chuffing out smoke from London to a track
and station closed decades ago. The rain
intensifies as memories flood back.

Hot water from a standpipe on the path
looping round rows of chalets, no-frills huts
usurped by high-tech mobile homes, this swathe
of giants' shoeboxes on metal struts.

Gone too the building where we breakfasted,
fluttering its galleon flag. A blaze
of speakered song plucked campers out of bed,
O what a beautiful morning!... As it was.

Mum's knack with thread and scissors meant we'd reap
honours at the Fancy Dress. I won
as a Pierrot, my sister as Bo Peep,
we paired as Robin Hood and Marion.

Rickety steps led down to golden sand,
the cliff so crumbly I could scrunch away
great chunks of ochre stuff in either hand.
All is sealed off by wire-mesh fence today.

QUICK AS A FLASH

Playground zoomings, muddied knees,
frogspawn, cycling with no brakes,
scrumping, skimming stones on lakes,
dangling upside-down in trees;

balanced eager at the top
of life's helter-skelter you
launched yourself to whoosh down through
promised thrills and spills non-stop.

No-one warned, or if they did
you weren't listening. Though it may
all still seem just yesterday
you're older now than Uncle Sid

doddering about back then.
Now foretellings, evidence
of things to come smite every sense,
swirl like a blizzard. Here again

you sit and wait, at intervals
bobbing out of little rooms
a file in hand, a doctor comes
peering left and right, and calls

a name: 'Anne Pretty!' 'Albert Gore!'
'Iris Speed!' 'Hugh Hope!' 'Jean Quick!' –
who's next to you. She grips her stick
and makes it wheezing to his door.

Some look absolutely crocked,
need arms or wheeling, fall asleep,
somehow get dealt with, but more keep
filtering in, all cruelly mocked

by magazines they're leafing through
stuffed with features on the young
and fit and beautiful, among
whom once… But now the call's for you…

The check finds nothing sinister
this time. You book the next, and get
out fast (your legs aren't rhubarb yet),
gratefully gulping down fresh air.

READING FRANCO SACCHETTI'S 'PASSANDO CON PENSIER PER UN BOSCHETTO'

Walking in thought through a wood you were ambushed
by those girls scrambling for flowers:
'Get that one! Get that!'
'Here it is! Here it is!'
'What is it, what is it?'
'It's a lily.'
'Go over there for violets!'
'Ow! how the thorns prick me!'

Maybe it never happened exactly like that,
in one luminous gush, like a fountain;
you shaped it over a desk, or pacing a loggia.
But there they were. 'Pick some rampions.'
'That's not it!' 'Yes it is!'
'Stay where you are for thyme.'
'She reaches in better than me.' Until,
'I can hear something in that bush.'
Pokings – and out glides a snake,
and as they flee, slipping and stumbling,
dropping their garlands, the rain comes down like a curtain.
Centuries ago.

Some perhaps died of plague, others no doubt
had children, then wizened into crones.
The flesh is long gone from the bone.

So far, and yet so near, those voices;
part of the living skein across times and places.

'Hey there, you! Come here for mushrooms!'

BLACK AND WHITE CHRISTMAS IN VERONA

I step out from the lift at the third floor,
turn left, thick carpeting beneath the case
I pull along ramifying corridor
hushes its wheels, in every recess

plumps a plush sofa, stands a vase of flowers.
My room-number at last. The train, long flight,
then taxi – I've been travelling many hours,
so quickly get to bed, switch off the light.

It had seemed a good idea to flee
England's crassness at this time of year,
its grabbing materialism, gluttony
and stupefaction, and so I've come here.

At breakfast the next day it seems I am
the only guest except for two obese
Germans making raids for yet more ham,
salami, fruit, rolls, butter, yoghurts, cheese.

'At what times do you serve your evening meal?'
'Just now,' the waiter replies, 'we're not.' 'But but,
surely this is a four-star hotel?'
'*Sì Signore*, but the restaurant is shut

in the evenings, most staff are away
enjoying a break,' he bobs down to retrieve
a dropped fork. 'That's what I've come for,' I say.
Outside looks cloudy. It is Christmas Eve.

I walk up past the Roman amphitheatre
rearing its arched tiers, the monument's
now the twenty-something-thousand seater
venue for summer musical events.

I dawdle around sight-seeing, the hours
fly in this grand and enchanting mix
of piazzas, loggias, palaces and towers,
I peer into courts, climb steps, my camera clicks;

I practise my Italian in a bar,
then settle in a dim-lit restaurant –
risotto, calamari, a guitar
softly twitters to a lilt of song.

Outside again, I'm buffeted by flurries
of thick snowflakes, O Noël, Noël!
A red-clad and white-bearded Santa scurries
past cursing. I reel into my warm hotel.

Christmas Day. The Germans have checked out.
The waiter smiles, 'Today, *signore*, the few
restaurants open will, I have no doubt,
have been booked full for months.' So what to do?

I eat a mighty breakfast, furtively
filch a fistful of bananas – they,
stuffed in my jacket as I leave my key,
are all the rest I'll have to eat today.

No snow is falling, but beneath my feet
scrunches the white quilt laid by last night's storm.
Shuttered shops, few people on the street.
Part half-believing, partly to get warm

I venture into churches. Services
enact themselves, glum and crepuscular;
priestly intonings, *l'Agnello* this,
Maria that, as if beamed down from far

intergalactic space. The gloomiest
of all is the Cathedral, frigid choir
and shuddering organ. Still, the soaring West
Front's Romanesque's worth turning to admire.

I cross the Adige by the arched stone bridge
the Romans built two thousand years ago;
the ancient parapet offers a ledge
to write my signature in fluffy snow.

Streets slope up to a commanding height
above the looping river; turning, I
look down on roofs, spires, bell-towers clad in white
spread beneath me under leaden sky.

But I've one more ecclesiastical
destination, lured there by its name,
San Tomaso Becket – once through all
Christendom our English martyr's fame

glowed inspirational. Now as I near
his church I'm lifted by a surf of noise,
choruses crescendoing. So here
at last's a place where worship can rejoice.

I tiptoe in to hover at the back –
but welcomes, hugs, handclasps draw me to
the heart of things. And every face is black
I realise, as I settle in a pew,

and all's going on in English. People sway
and whirl in vivid garments in the aisles,
fervour buzzes when they sing or pray,
they turn to greet each other, flashing smiles.

The service over, I stay on to bask
in so much warmth and friendliness. I feel
sure if they knew my plight they would all ask
me back to share a family Christmas meal.

Edward, the priest, explains his congregation
are workers from Nigeria and Ghana.
Fruit cramming my pockets flicker the temptation:
'Would you perhaps care for a banana?'

But no! – that's what our English football thugs
lob to black players... Still, I wish I could,
as I depart accepting yet more hugs
have something to give back in gratitude.

Piazza dei Signori – and I nod
to Dante's statue, sprinkled with fresh snow.
Who vivified pain wrought by his harsh God
while here in exile, centuries ago.

VANTAGE POINT

Swallows twitter past my open window,
veering to the cathedral's crenellations;
from the square below the fountain lifts
its tiers of basins, topped by a rearing centaur.

Two small girls dressed in red cavort around it
and from the Corso a brass band
turns in and halts, emblazoning the twilight.
Mythologies and saints, baroque and Gothic.

Beyond the opposite roofs the land drops sheer
to bays and grottoes, the blue sea
across which ancient Greeks came colonising,
where now as then tuna are leaping.

Dark comes, and stars above the *passeggiata*,
the bars and ceramics shops. Out there
on unknown planets hydrothermal vents
seethe generating life…

This vantage point chanced into holds
near and far in balance and perspective,
ballast to carry with me when I go.
Behind me from the kitchen the fridge chuckles.

THE LETTERS

More than the photographs
cramming my albums of
twenty-plus years ago,
Antrim's strands and cliffs,
the swing of your blonde hair
beside a waterfall
or over your red car,
it is this slender sheaf
of letters, words acute
and tender in that blue
script that arrests me now
all you once embraced,
every mortal cell,
has died and been replaced;
but most of all to know
as I hold each sheet
that your hand once lay
and moved here is what grips
a vice around my ribs.

THE LAST CHILD OF EMPIRE

Lined up on playground asphalt by
fussing teachers, told to stop
fidgeting, we stared at sky
while the flag was hoisted up;
then the Headmaster's reedy voice
picturing places far away
bound by ties we should rejoice
to honour thus on Empire Day.

Feet aching, I was well aware
my parents were against all this:
conquering others, taking their
stuff, making them work for us.
Not that it had ever done
our sort any favours, that
Empire 'upon which the sun,'
as they put it, 'never set.'

It shone here, when it did, on scarred
streets, choked bomb-sites; all was drab,
make-do, hand-me-down, and tired.
On the fishmonger's sluiced slab
flopped congregations of dead fish;
I watched a pear-shaped wrecking-ball
swinging from a crane to smash
the air-raid shelter on Oak Hill.

And yet, I felt a guilty thrill
knowing that I was a part
of something so enormous, all
that paraphernalia, at its heart
this England that they still called 'home'
on outback farms, in clamorous
bazaars, plantations. Ancient Rome
had never been a patch on us.

The first cartoon I could recall
showed Europe morphed into a swart
swastika-blazoned crocodile:
artistic licence could distort
Scandinavia stretched above
and Spain and Portugal beneath
our island to the likeness of
gaping jaws with sabre teeth.

That we'd not been swallowed was
something to do with all those far
places rallying to our cause;
from Alice Springs to Zanzibar,
logging camps and desert tents,
atolls, shearing-sheds and kraals,
all creeds and colours – an immense
body with a single pulse.

Many of my childhood books
were set in India, elephants
with howdahs bobbing on their backs,
bright screeching birds and jungle plants,
as much as English rivers, woods,
red pillar-boxes, were what we were;
Mowgli nodded to Robin Hood,
the Ghats rolled down to Lincolnshire.

The coins that bore King George's head
still had 'Ind. Imp.' round the edge
as all that title vaunted slid
off the cliff: we'd lost the Raj.
They didn't like or want us. All
I knew was wrong or obsolete.
We'd no bananas, but we'd still,
I gloried, the world's biggest fleet.

We were the last to grow inside
a scheme of things already gone,

fossil images; the tide
of history went thundering on,
mobs, demagogues, guerrilla war –
those we'd done little good now meant
to get their lands back. England swore,
tried vain reprisals, packed, and went;

liberating them into,
too often, native tyrannies.
Meanwhile we groped to find a new
role shorn of all I'd mesmerise
myself by garbling, the whole show
for which we traipsed from desks to stand
where those born since can never go,
in the playground of a Promised Land.

THE SUMMER OF THE WORLD CUPS

The year we staged all those World Cups
had not had much to do outdoors. We kicked
a ball in streets clear of parked cars, pausing
to let the occasional vehicle murmur through,
climbed hoardings, frittered about.
Sundays were worst, everything was shut
except the newsagent's, where Bert Drain lounged
gobbing at bikes propped at the kerb,
his aim, his game, to land it on their saddles,
he'd thought up a system for a World Cup at this.
In the doorway a paper-rack wheezed
in breeze which raised a spiral of dust waltzing
around the pavement, the liveliest thing in sight.

We went to the park. On the way, for a thrill
you could balance along the six-inch-wide parapet
of the footbridge over the railway cutting,
a forty-foot drop, one slip and you were dead.
And on the putting-green we'd lift a club
and lash the ball miles off the course, or send it
ripping through flowerbeds reaping petals.
'Oy! Oy! Oy!' yelled Charlie, the park-keeper.
So we went to the swings, and he followed
to chuck us out for being too old:
'"Under Twelve" it says there! Can't you read?'

We could read. In the park's little branch-library
we found a copy of Gogol's *Dead Souls*,
in Russian, never taken out.
We took it out, and a Russian-English dictionary,
and set to work. By the time we reached word twelve,
each having so many alternative meanings,
we had sheets of variant translations,
it looked like the genealogical tree
of some rampant family. If we slogged on
to the end we'd have more English-language versions

than there are atoms in the cosmos, and would
have been dead for aeons. We took it back.
But kept the dictionary, went with it up
the High Street and into shops
jabbing at pages, jabbering broken English,
'*Da, da!* We are Russian tourists!' They threw us out.

So it was just as well I commandeered
Aunt Flo's clapped-out tennis rackets,
in her hall-stand for years with the umbrellas,
last used when long skirts swept grass courts.
Their wooden handles had strange grooves and knobs,
strings were slack, bust, missing.
We invented 'hoccis' with these things for sticks,
jackets thrown down for goalposts, the game's rules:
you could only run with the ball while flipping it up,
and for just five touches, and no head-high scythings.

That summer there'd been the first World Cup
to enthral the nation, being on television,
which we'd not got, but a friend of Mum's had one.
On her little black-and-white screen
I'd seen, beamed all the way from Switzerland,
silky Latino skills, the Uruguayans
dump England out, Max Morlock's hat-trick,
then in the Wankdorf Stadium final his West Germans
filch the trophy from the magical Magyars.

There had to be a Hoccis World Cup.
Our pitch was bounded on one side by path,
the other touchline billowed out past trees,
was negotiable. We decided
that teams had seven players, so as there were
just five of us a match required
doubling-up: as Köhlhever I dinked
the tennis-ball cross-field to Launmauer
(me too) who hoicked it to Kurt Nodd
(Mick, who played for our school hockey team)

whose shot was brilliantly saved by
the Soviet goalie Schlobberdevodka (Chris).
Half the fun was making up the names,
Kikyu and Kursyu (Japan), Mustapha Fag
of Turkey, the Polish, skippered by Bkskrtcz,
couldn't muster a single vowel between them.
We sustained a running commentary
so we knew what was happening, and refereed it,
coming down hard on shirt-tugging Italians.

We got through dozens of World Cups,
skipping meals, playing on through dusk.
'Oy! Oy! Oy!' Charlie emerged from his hut
prancing about whirling his hand-bell
until his peaked cap fell off, hollering
'Closing time! Everyone out!'
Futile. Locking the gates couldn't shut the park,
the iron railings that once topped its low wall
had been carted away during the War
to make into bombs to drop on Berlin.

But school resumed and darkness closed round indoor
Meccano evenings, bolting plates, juggling cogs,
board games – Buccaneer and Cluedo.

And when again days lengthened into Spring,
the girls came, white socks bobbing over the grass
from the Long Lane corner, to meet us at the park shelter.
The Brazilian and German stars, wily Abracadabra,
the Gold Coast's Mbang twins, and the rest of the greats
had no more outings, their rackets hung up for ever.
A curtain drawn, a new world opening.

Leaving an afterglow, golden goals,
that run timed perfectly to meet the cross
and my volley bursting the roof of the notional net.
Nothing then foreseen surpassing it.

BIRTHDAY POEM

>For Christopher Speake

You've marshalled your thought, magisterially brought
    your case to its climax – then, *Hell!*
you exclaim, *It's absurd, I just can't find the word
    I know I know perfectly well!*

It's slipped without trace; this is often the case,
    you say, these days. *Nominal aphasia*
is the medical phrase, when you meet only haze
    where words once were. And it could get crazier:

You might end mumbling *Hollow thing lifted to swallow
    runny stuff,* where you used to say cup
of tea; or *stick scratches on card strip for matches.*
    You think that I'm sending you up?

Yes, the core's still intact, stuffed with useless old fact,
    the monarchs of England in order,
names of World War II ships, dates of Wolves' championships –
    the blips encroach from the border.

Yet since most lives are cursed with so much of the worst
    it may be sweet relief to go gaga,
brain-blizzards not knowing who's coming or going
    around the grim close of one's saga.

But I mock you enough, black humour's no stuff
    for a birthday – my role perhaps is,
born four days before you, to reassure you:
    age has nothing to do with your lapses.

I too started to wonder when having searched under
    the wardrobe, the bed, round the floor
for my slippers I found them both safe and sound
    on my feet. But we've been there before.

At our primary school, where we both played the fool,
    I remember Benetto, the Beak,
when you came in again with no satchel, in pain
    grating, *Next you'll forget your head, Speake!*

Once when you called after breakfast, Mum's laughter
    flummoxed you, till she said,
*My day-dreaming son, his paper-round done,
    thinks it's night, he's undressed, gone to bed.*

What in youth were engaging quirks we fear as *ageing*
    now. But there's no need for panic.
Likewise some young wanker has dubbed as *cantankerous*
    all in us once hailed as *dynamic*.

THIS LIFE

Dangling from low boughs plump lemons bobble
against my forehead as I cross the garden

to breakfast, cheese, ham rolls, an apple, coffee.
I stroll through sunshine to the Y-shaped jetty.

Our boat zips round sheer cliffs, bobs into grottoes,
drops anchor in a little bay, the woman

next to me slabbers sun-cream on her husband,
he hippo-flops into the turquoise water

so half of it leaps up towards the headland
strewn with stone rings, the prehistoric village.

Today, *lo zuzzurellone*, just too loopy
for work, he gets the bus to Quattropani,

looped by butterflies plucking fruits and flowers
he beams at walkers, '*Sono zuzzurellone.*'

A swish of warm air twists up a dropped crisp-bag
against the ancient blocks of the Greek tower

incorporated in the Spanish ramparts.
Between the two, things happened: sackings, slaughters.

A bar by moonlit sea, a guitar twanging.
This life... If only... But for now, each morning

lemons bobbing round my head like clustered
galaxies come down in benediction.

Note: *zuzzurellone*, the final word in the Italian dictionary, is designated 'regional', and defined as 'a playful person', 'a child-like person'.

RUNNER

Feet padding up behind me, fast, and coming
abreast he slows, turns to me: twenty-ish,
just thin white shorts and vest against the wintry
sift of rain along the river footpath.
'Which way should I head to reach the airport?'
'At the next bridge go up to the road, turn right,'
I detail junctions, veers, 'then from the Greyhound
keep right on out to the ring-road, cross it,
it's two miles further.'
                     Rather him than me.
'Thanks.' He scuds off into twilight under
bare trees lurched at the water's edge as if
stunned in mid-spasm, clutching at thin air.

Then it comes back: how once I did all this,
and daily, training, how you bowl along
gulping lungfuls, the world spinning beneath
your feet and streetlamps flicking overhead,
reeling in distance, home with all that time
for evenings deep in books, or seeing friends.

How has time got so much less? Why have I never,
and now never shall, become…
                           But it's not those
far-flung goals all around ambition's compass
that ail me, but things missed out near-at-hand.

Leaves lie shoaled, and as I've not since childhood
I stoop, scoop up an armful, glistening, rustling,
then shudder with the pang of realising
I cannot name the trees above them. Rain
fresh as ever on my cheeks, my hands
let their freight splash gently back to earth
they've rarely dug, and never made a garden.

OFF THE BRINK

I hit the ground sprawling but, prepared for that,
bounce up unscathed and striding, feel the zing
and blood-surge that repays launch-off.

Down the open stretch below the summit,
stones scuttering from my boots, I'd known I'd veered
astray from where I'd left the path through forest

that wound me up, but known I'd intersect it
so pushed on to this brink near twice my height
above it, sat legs dangling, jumped.

In the afterglow the question flickers,
*Should I be doing this, 800 metres
up, and no-one within sound or sight?*

Through foliage blue shreds of sea,
alongside a luxuriance of bush
sluiced with gold. Then slowly taking in –

a rift not crossed on the way up, stacked logs,
hints opening ahead – a colder thrill:
that this I'm on is not the path I thought it.

GETTING THERE

From all I'd heard it wasn't far, but far
enough to need some forethought and a map.
And yet these got me not exactly nowhere
but nowhere nearer, whatever the signage promised
roads veered astray to blight or blank horizons,

I tried the river path, out of the hubbub
a few steps down beside the bridge you're strolling
past willows trailing in water, ducks to feed
and people walking dogs, and every spring
fresh bursts of daffodils.
      But the path ends,
and though a boat might drift me vaguely further
pleasurable loitering felt by now
a kind of truancy. I came back up.

One day that rattletrap old train pulled in,
I climbed aboard, a whistle blew along
the platform and we ambled into a branch-line
I had thought closed down decades ago
goutiing white steam. 'For Adlestrop,' some said,
or Shangri-la.
    Nothing where I alighted
except a stile, the track up to the ridge:

sunstruck, assuaging, it lay spread before me.